"Illustrations & Art works
by Eve Harrison"

Compiled by Philip R. Harrison

Illustrations & Paintings by Louise Harrison
Copyright©EveHarrison2014

First Edition

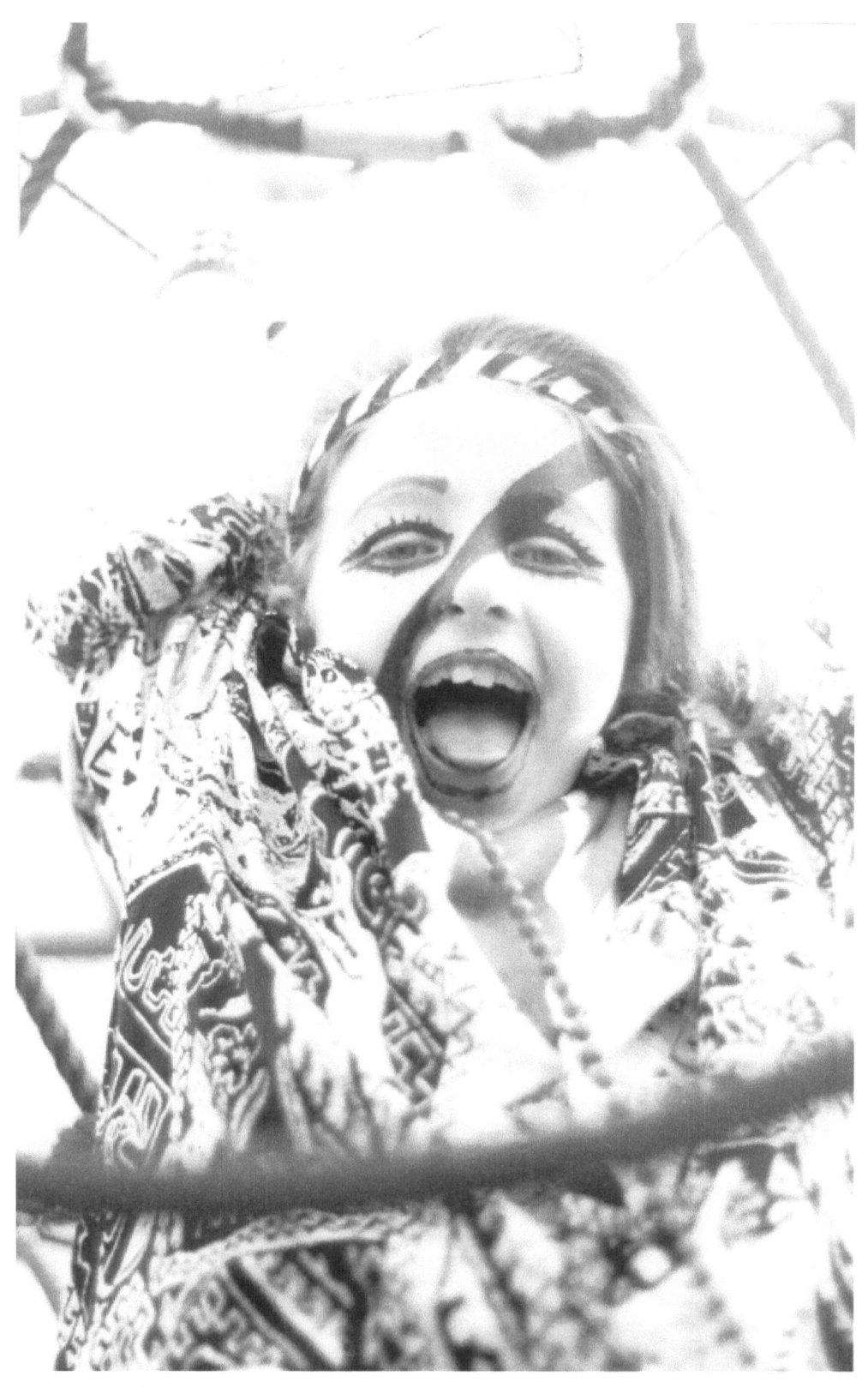

Eve Harrison 1990

Travel together into another mind.

A paranoid schizophrenic mind.

Now you can see imagination from inside us. Walking another path.

From blackness to another sun.

And before tomorrow starts the fight again.

I'm walking among the birds
and treesand I can hear the
windmovethe leaves. I feel glad
I am alone. No one can see me,
No one can notice, chase me and
Kill me. When I walk with fear
Inside the fear can stay behind.

In a room with us in chairs

on a ward called a prison

voices talk from space and I listen

but physical in ways. We are

stars from science fiction.

Forms of creatures and aliens.

We can defeat them.

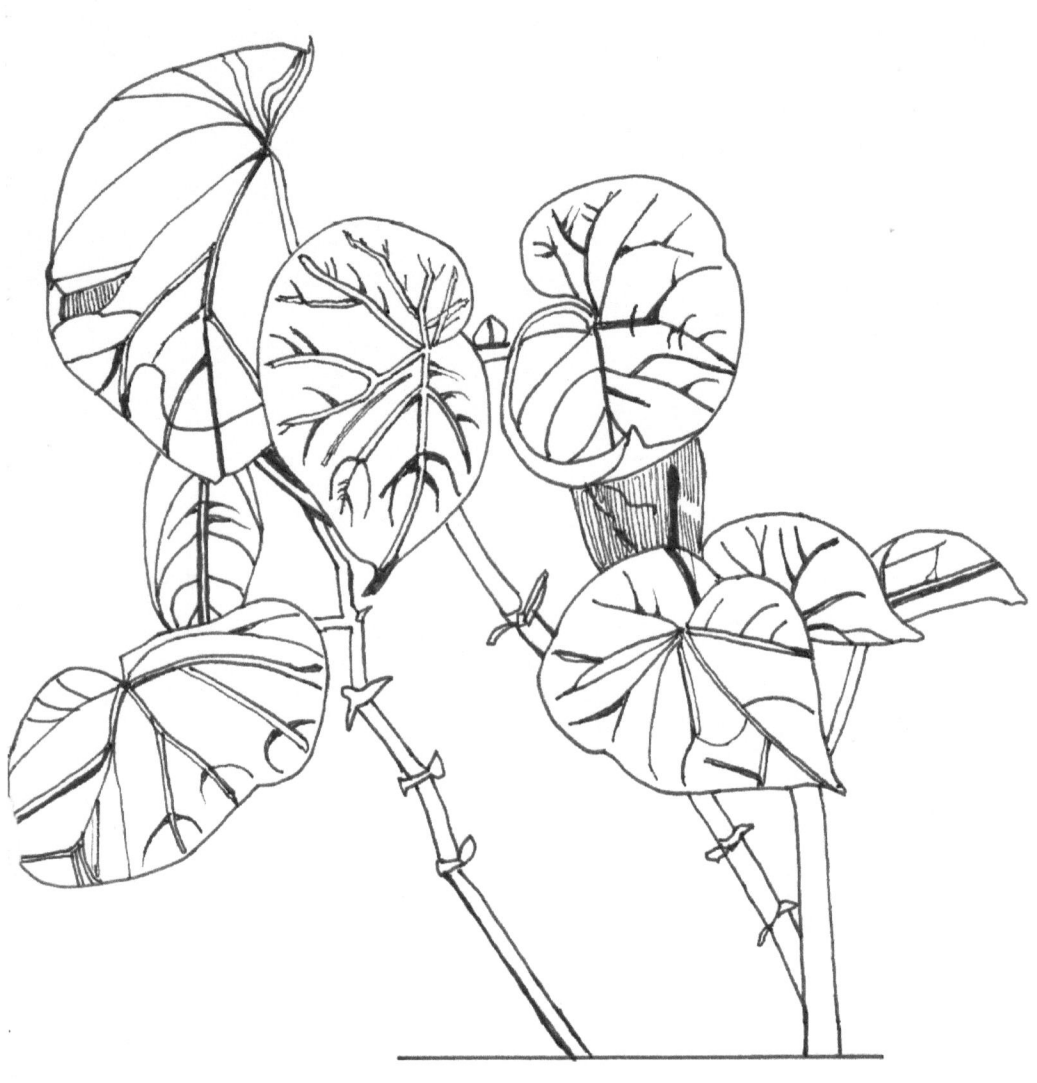

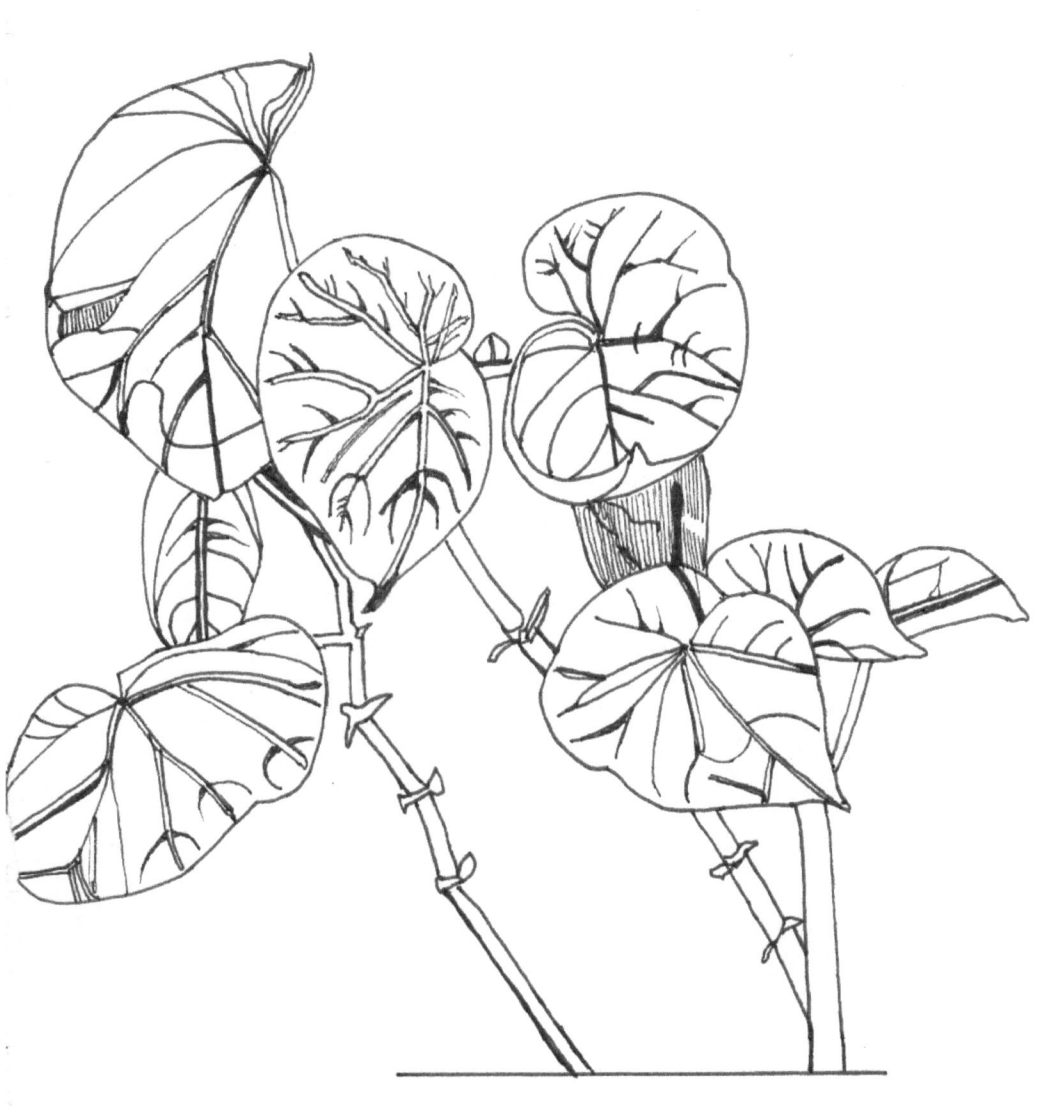

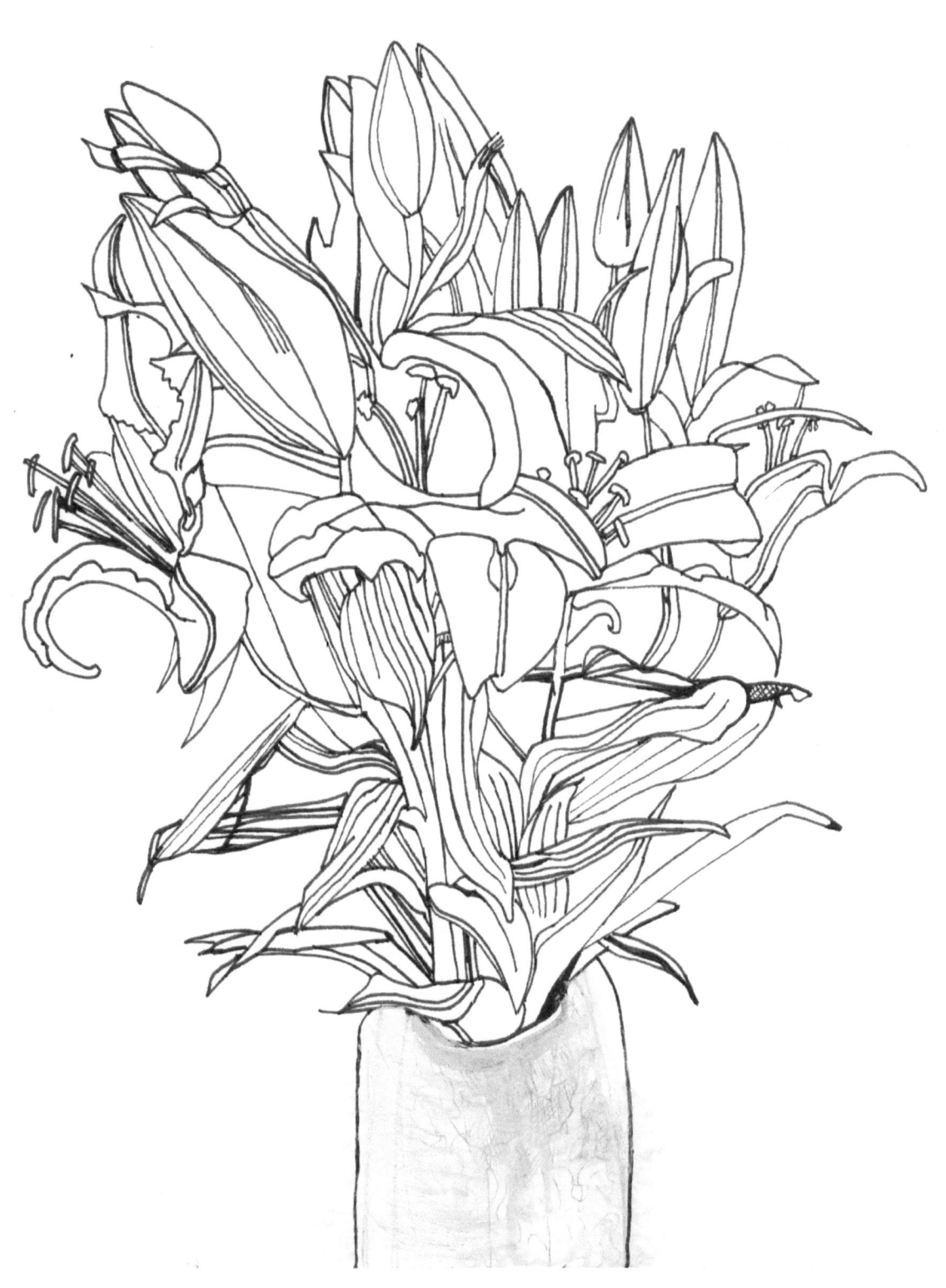

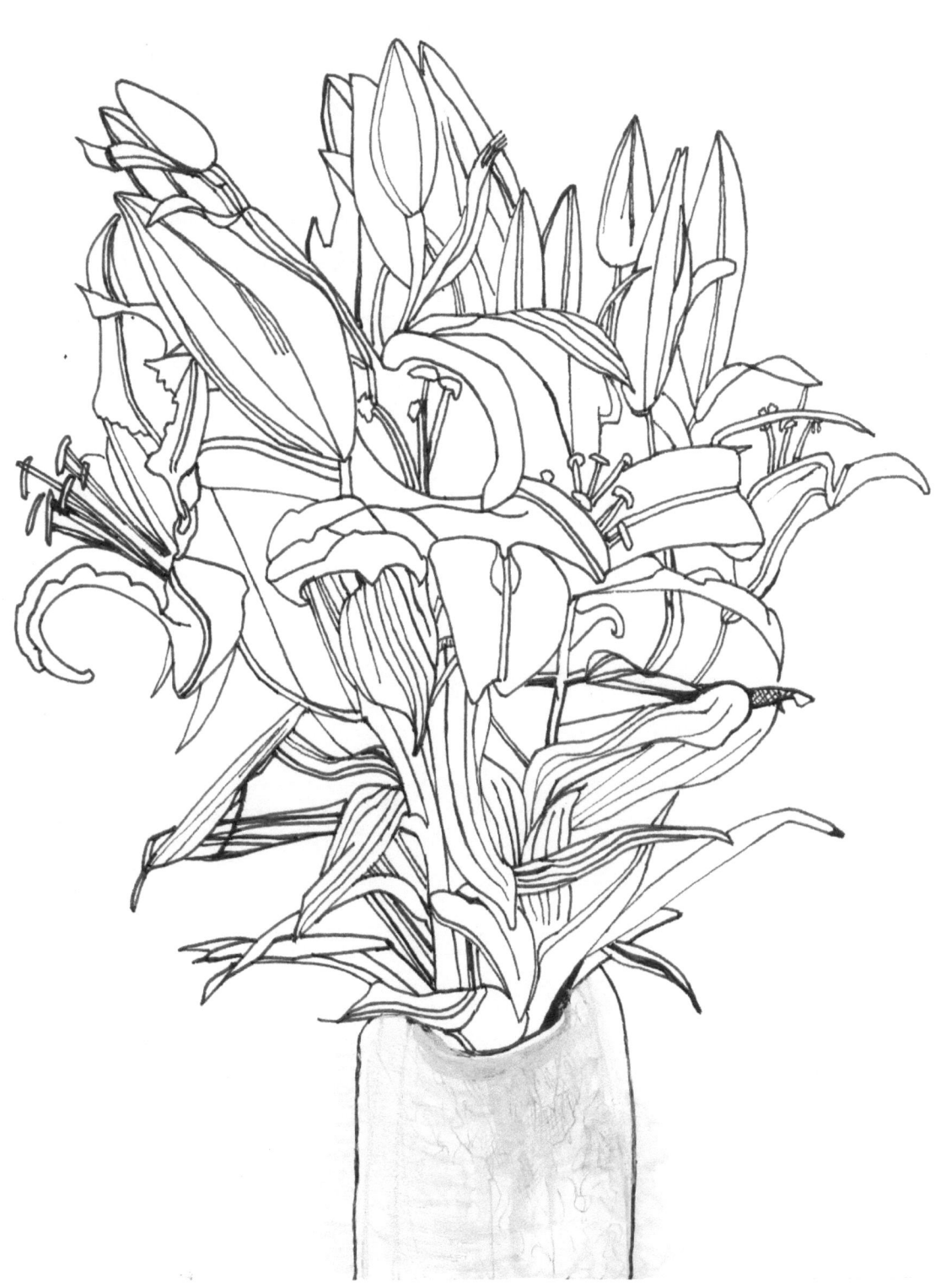

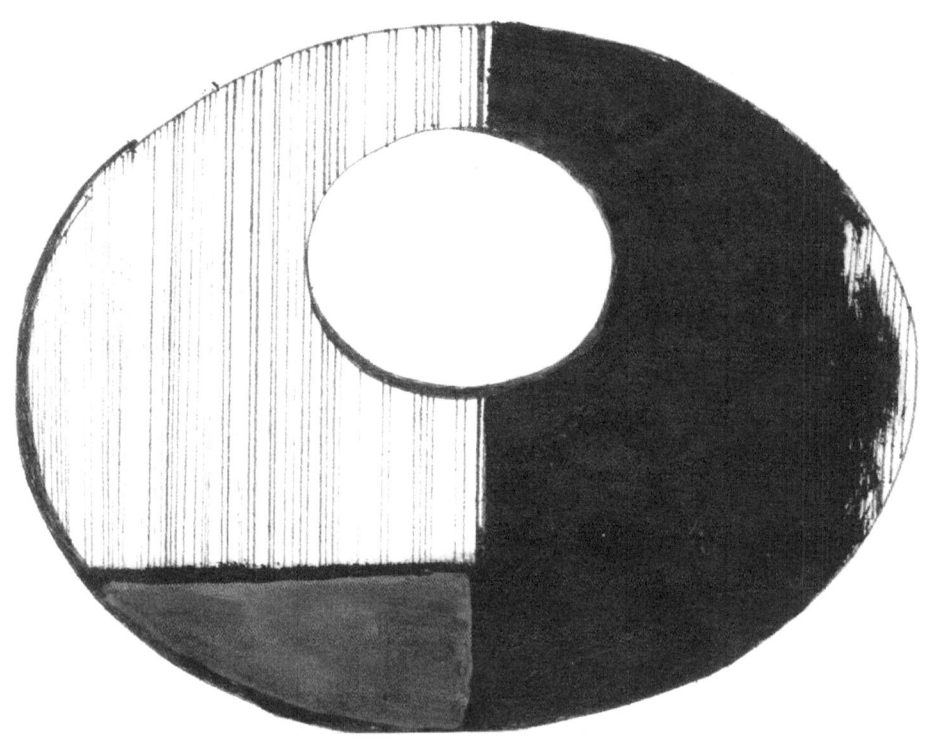

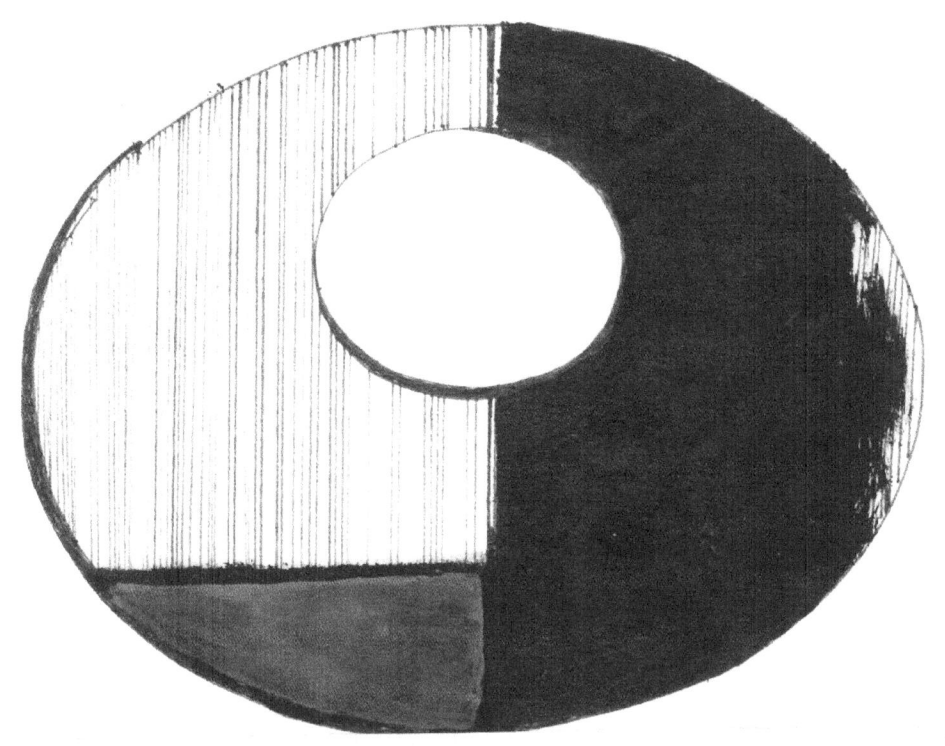

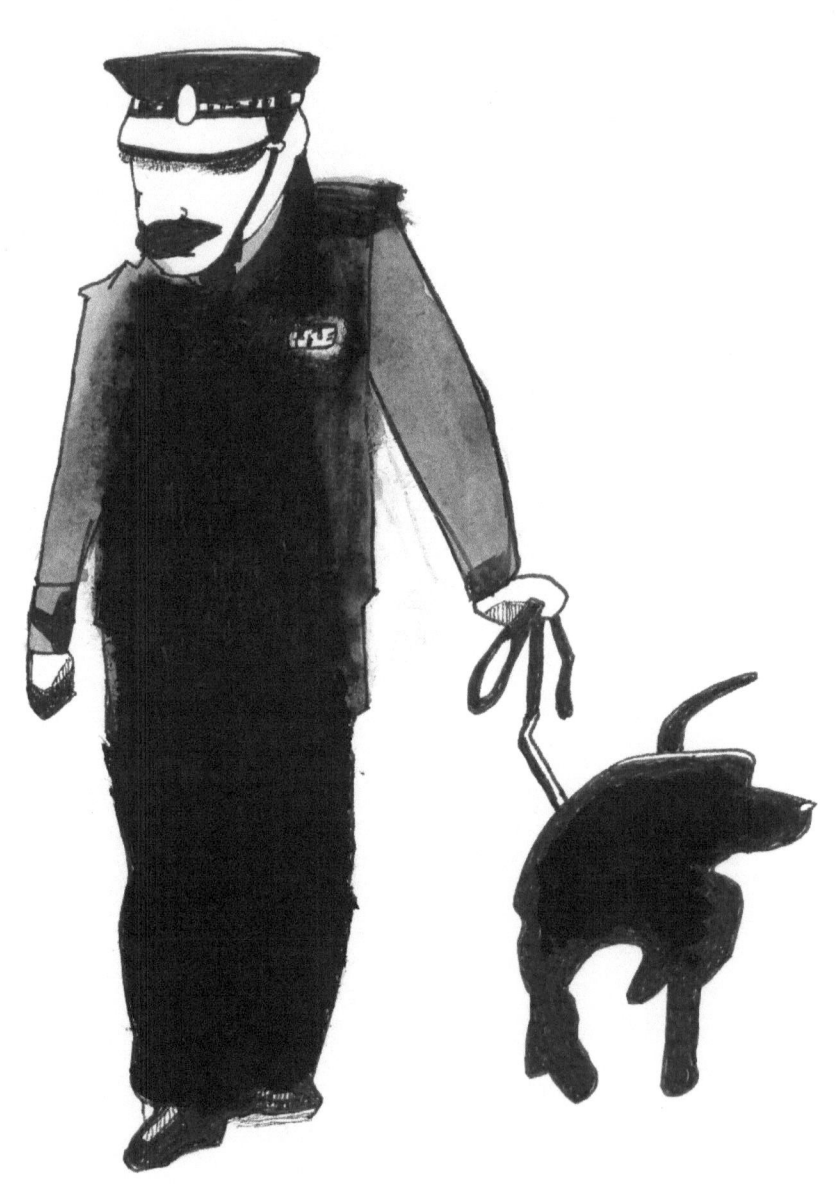

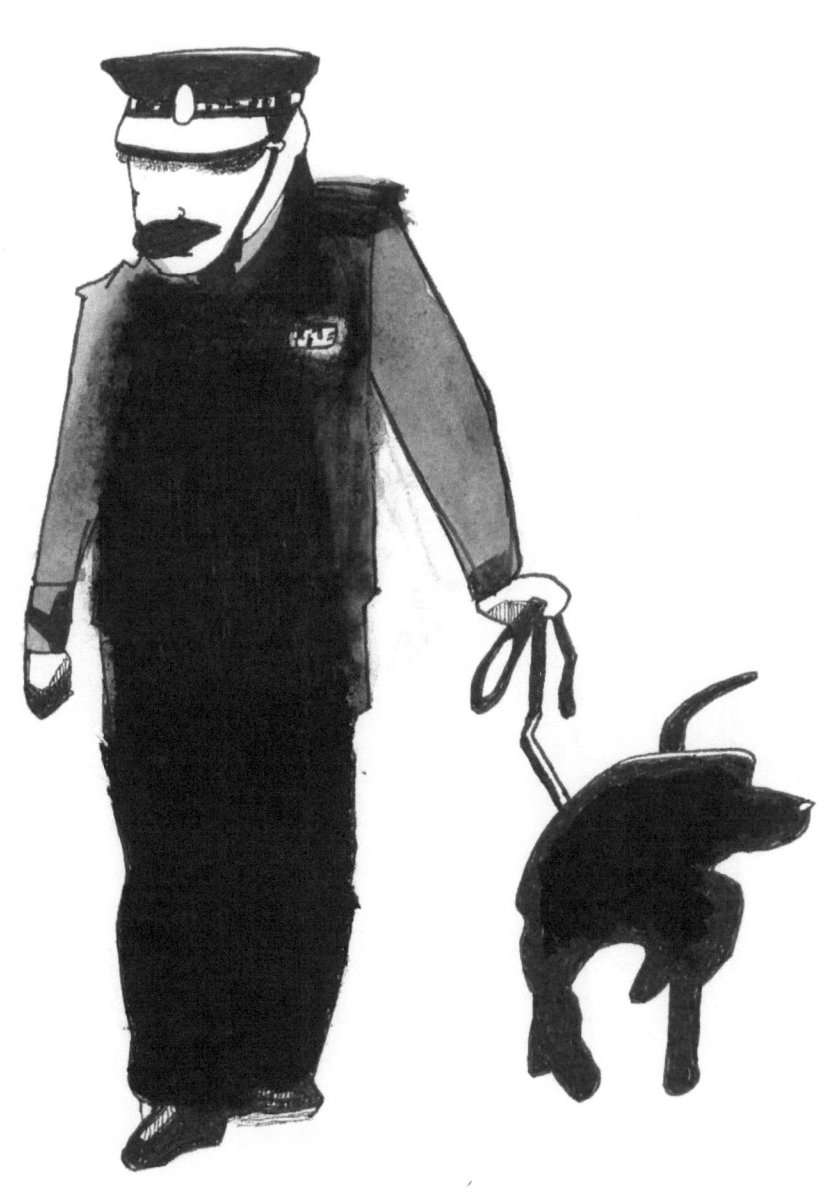

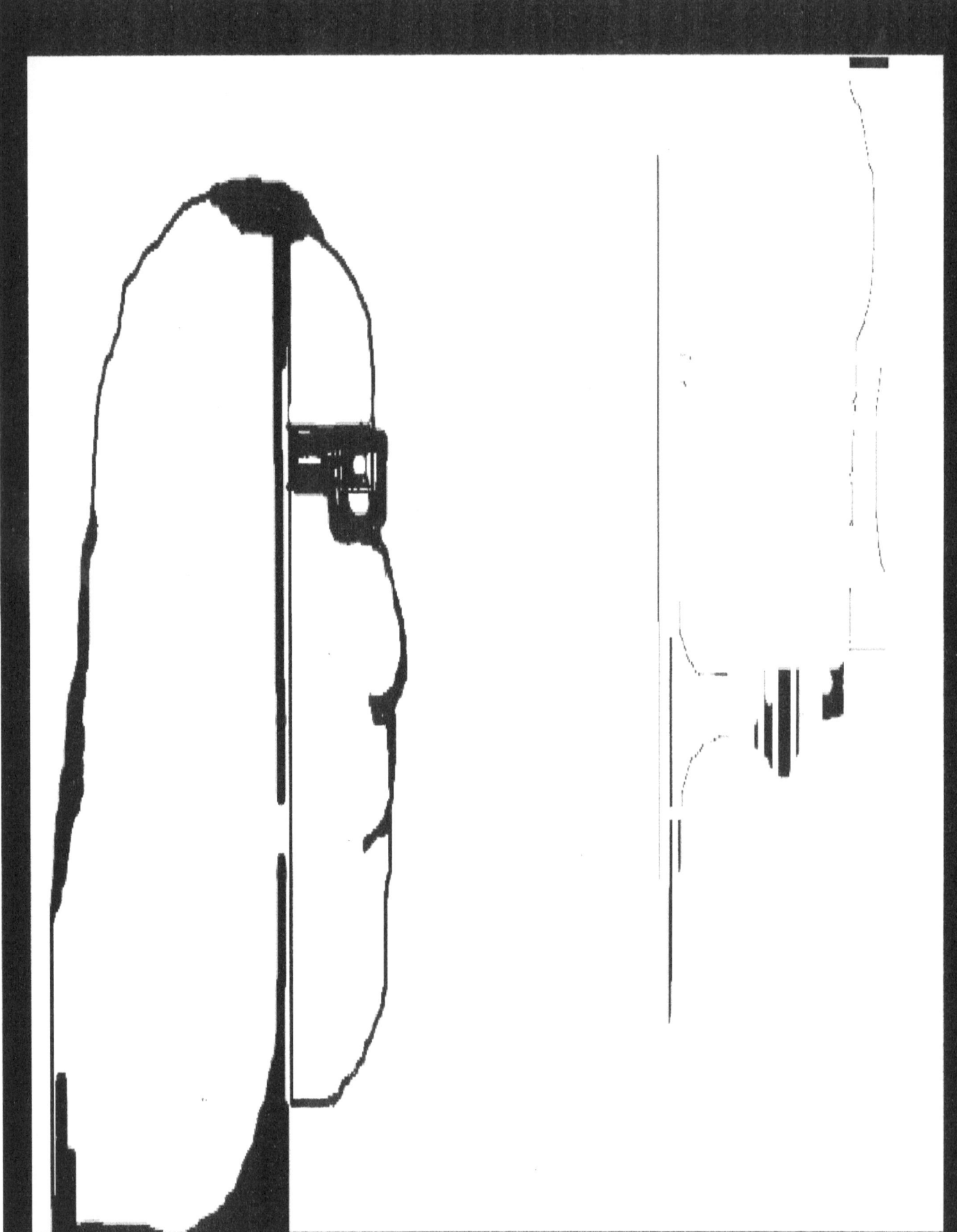

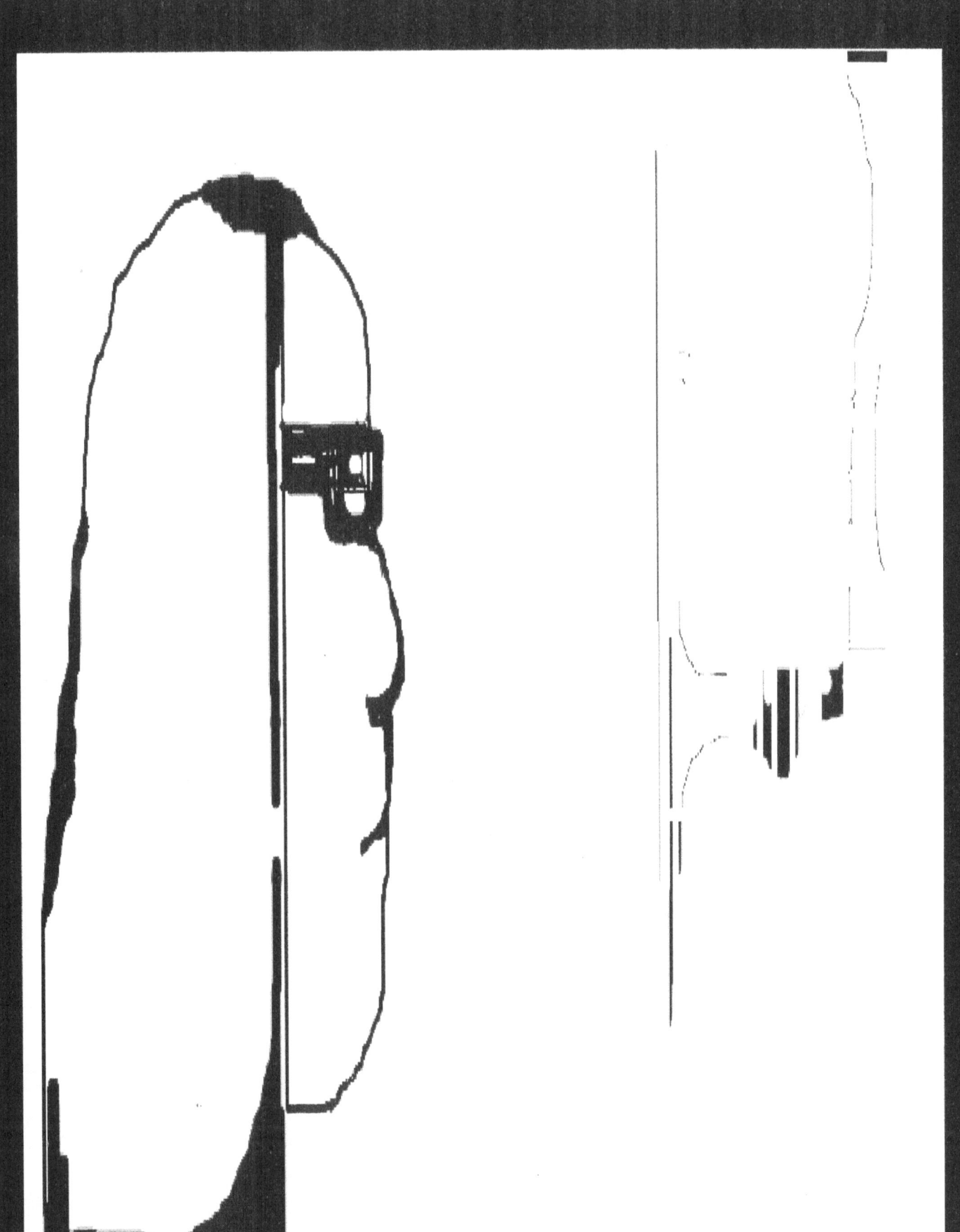

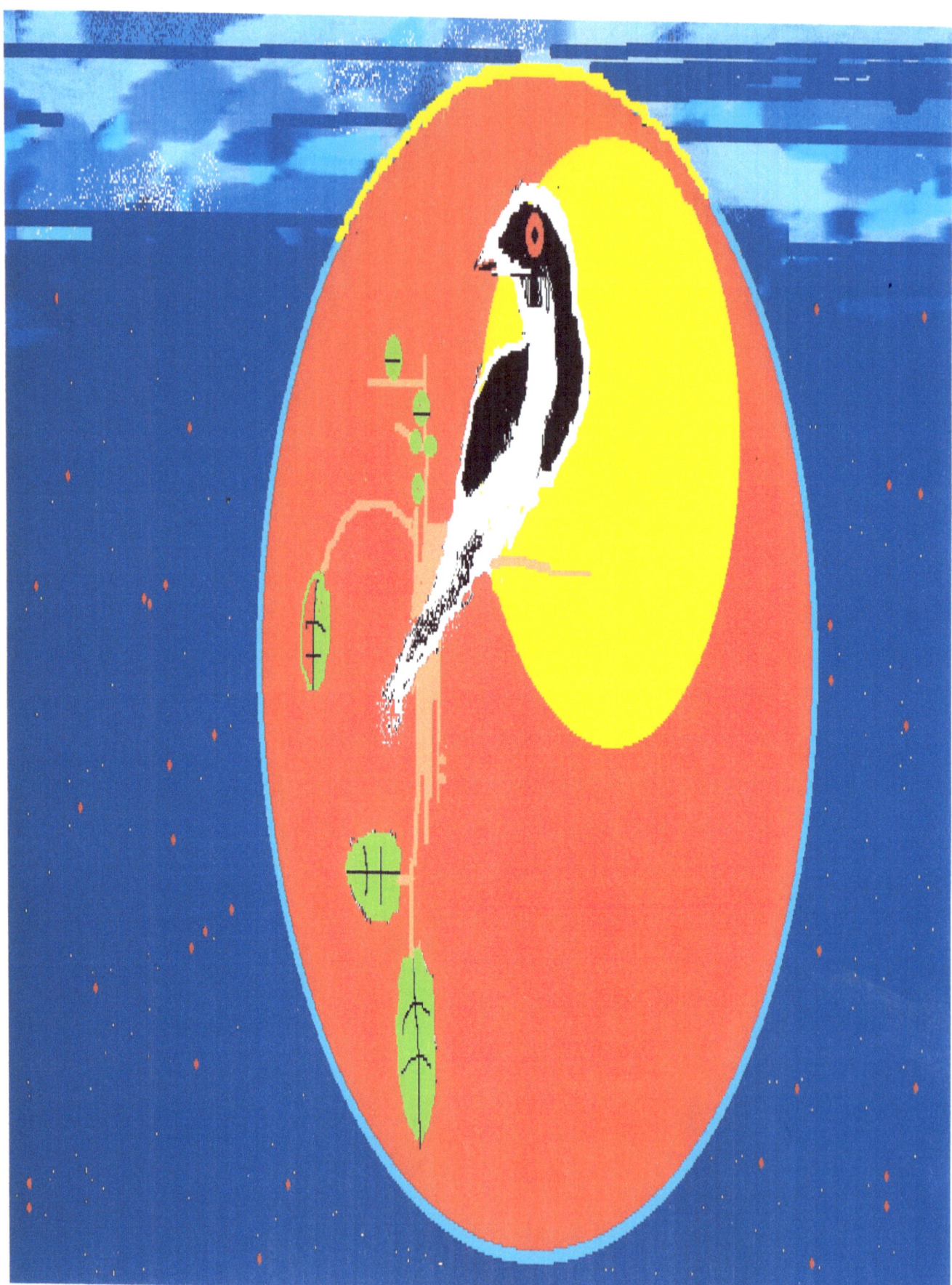

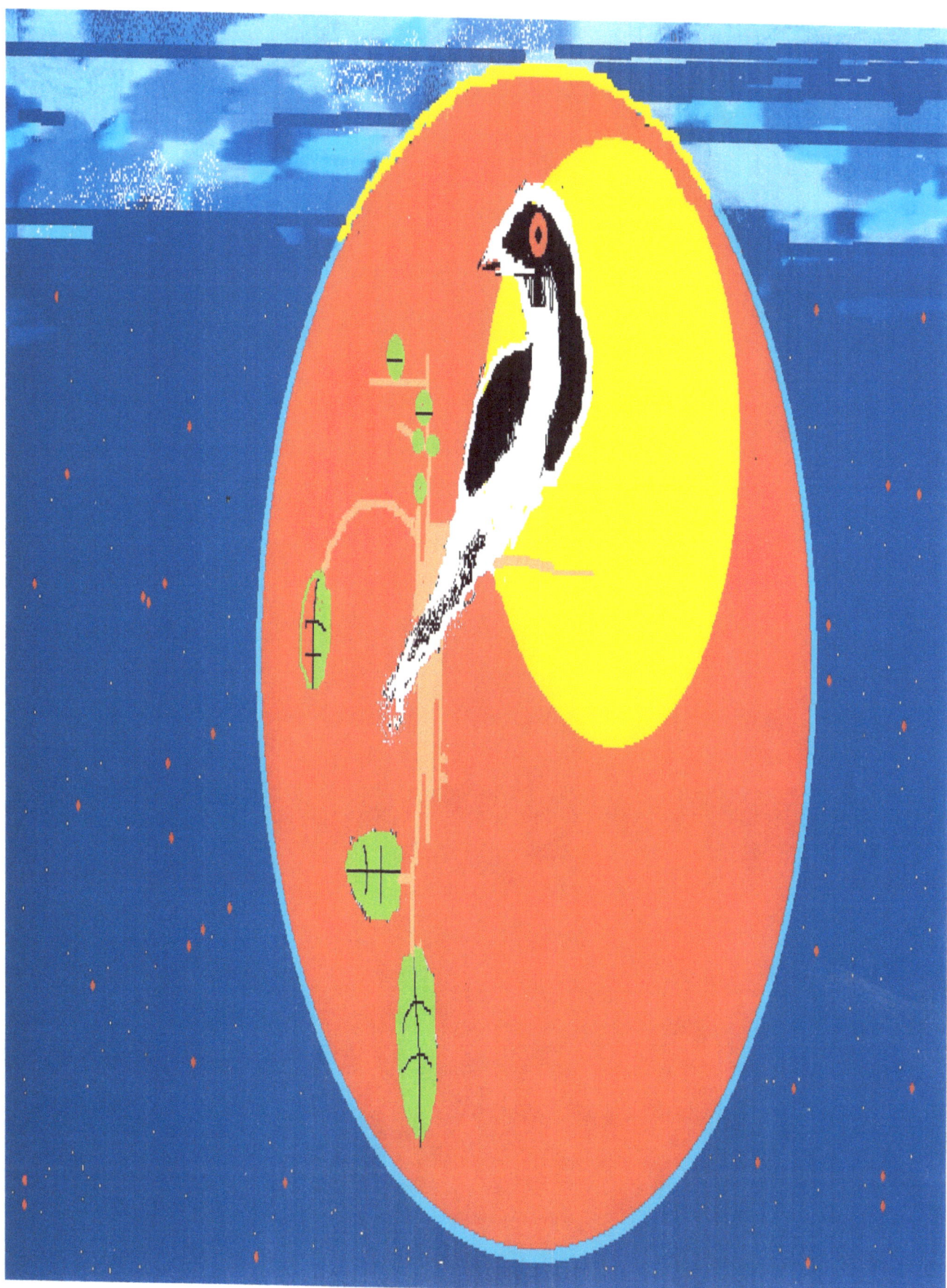

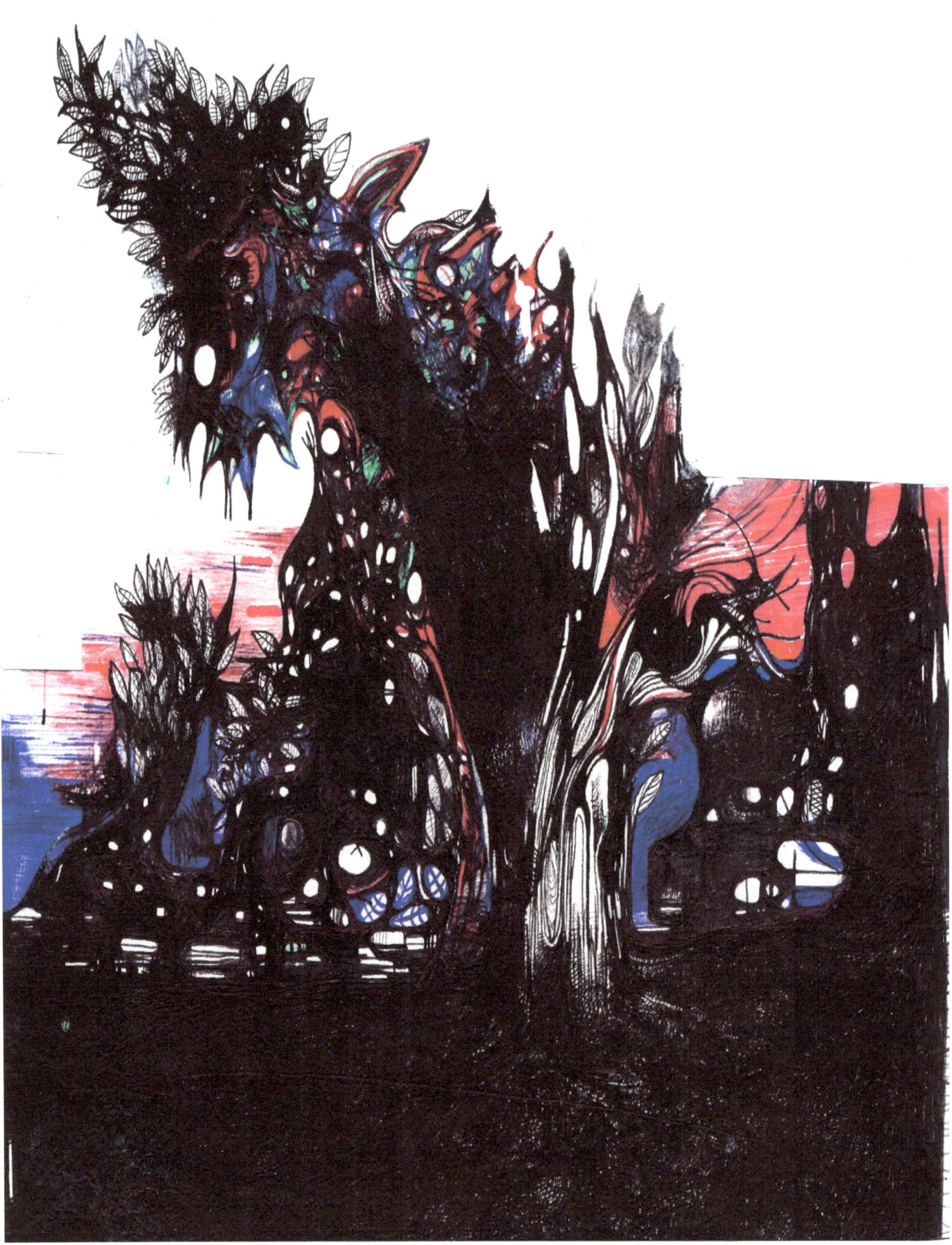

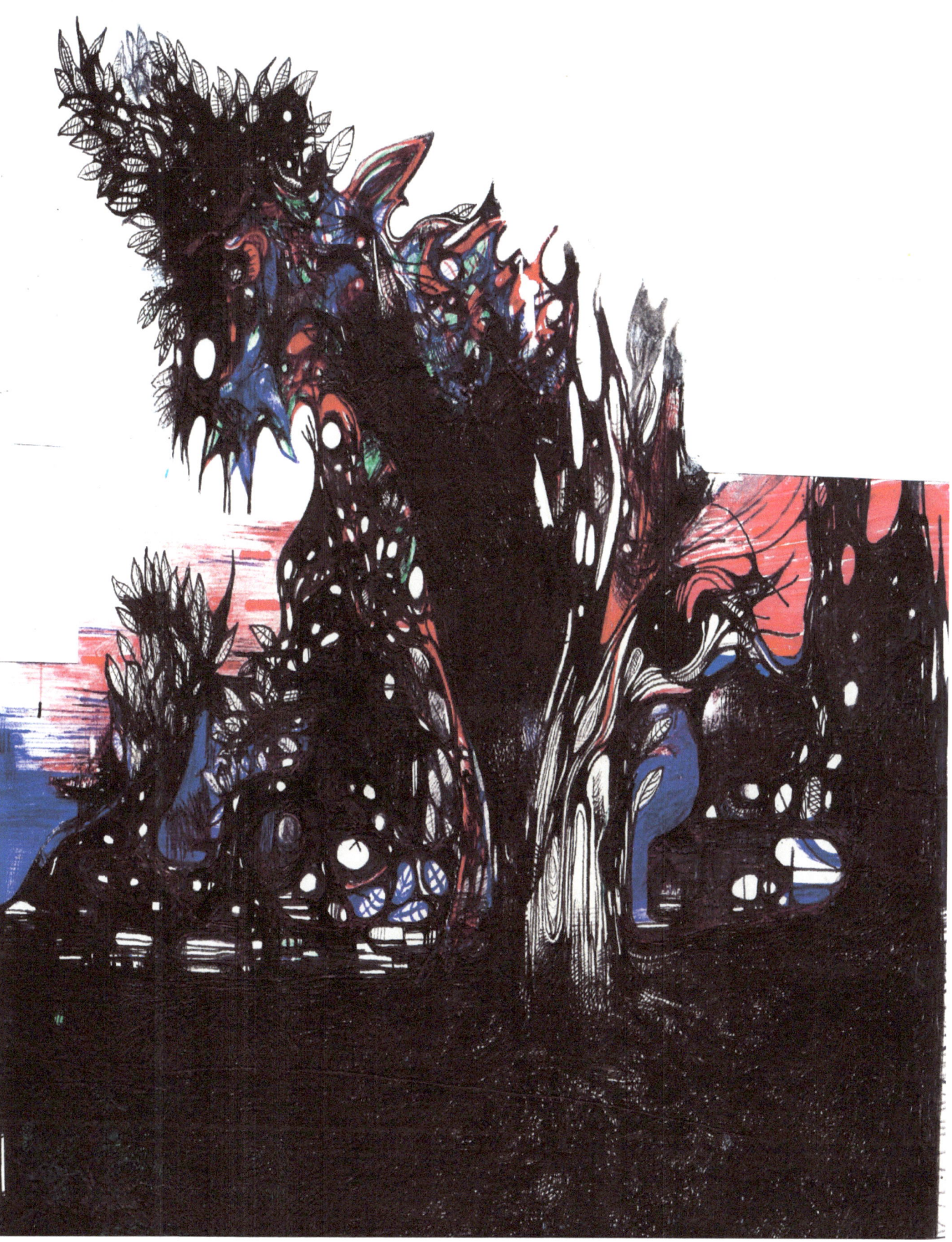

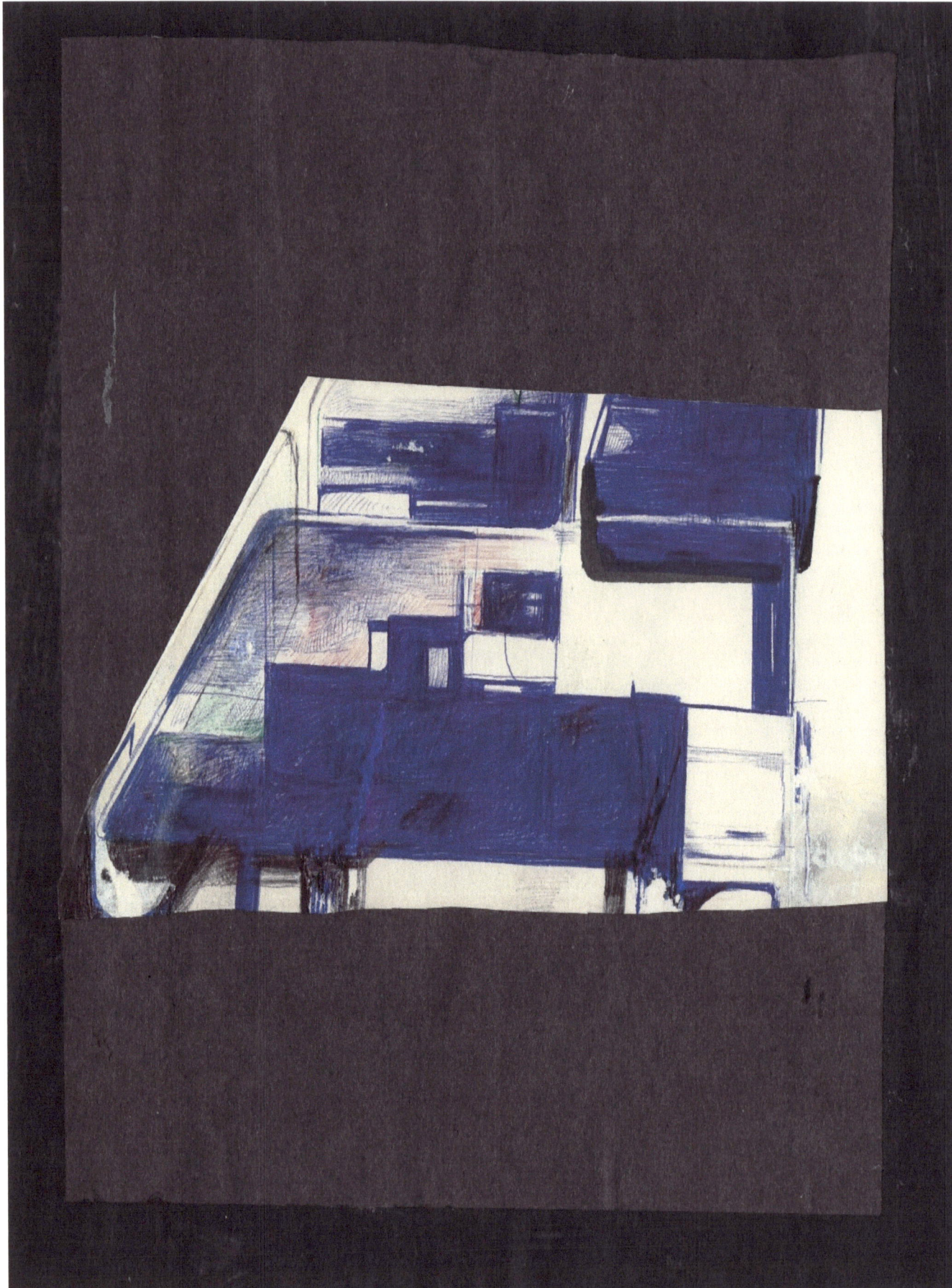

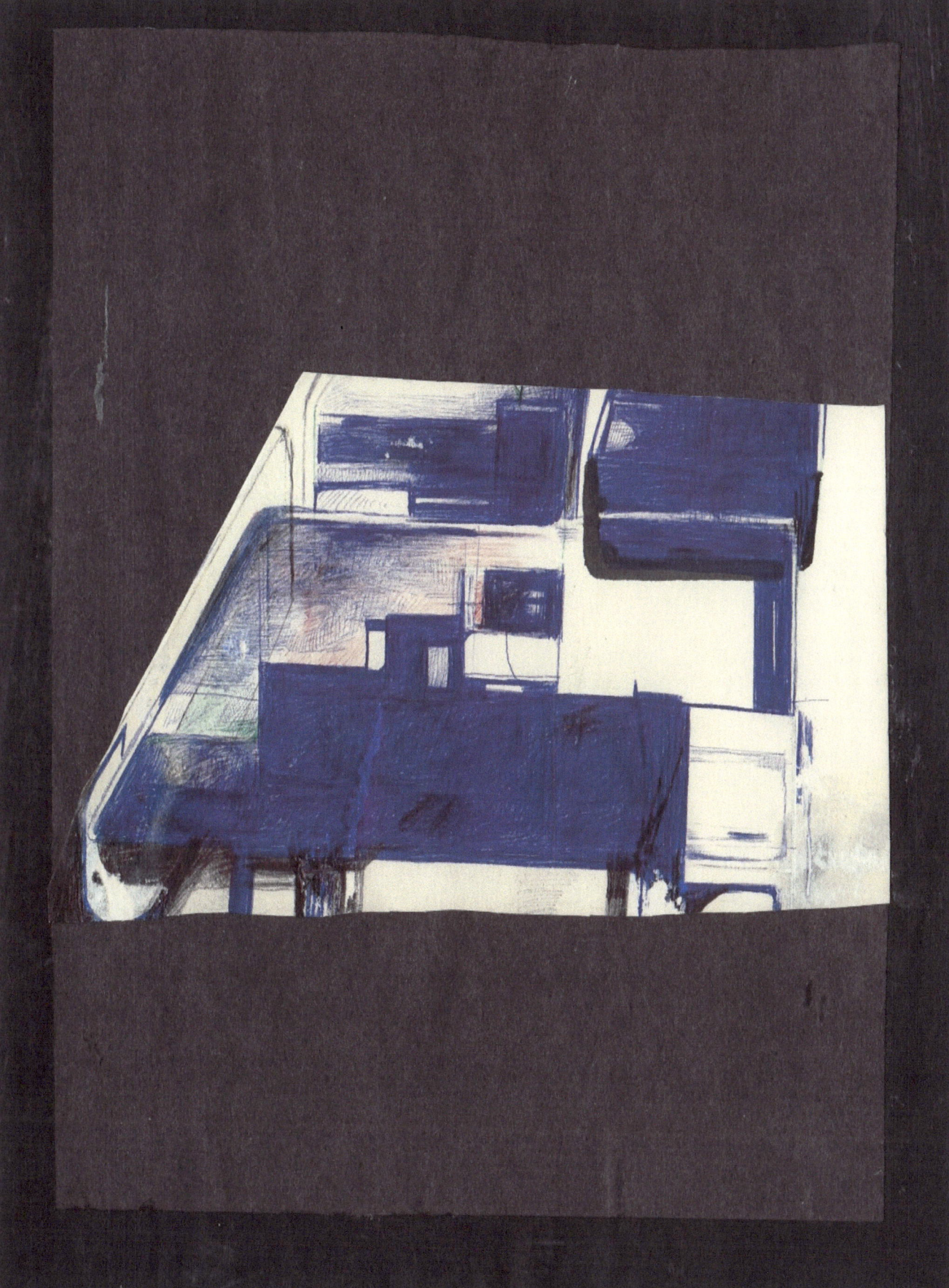

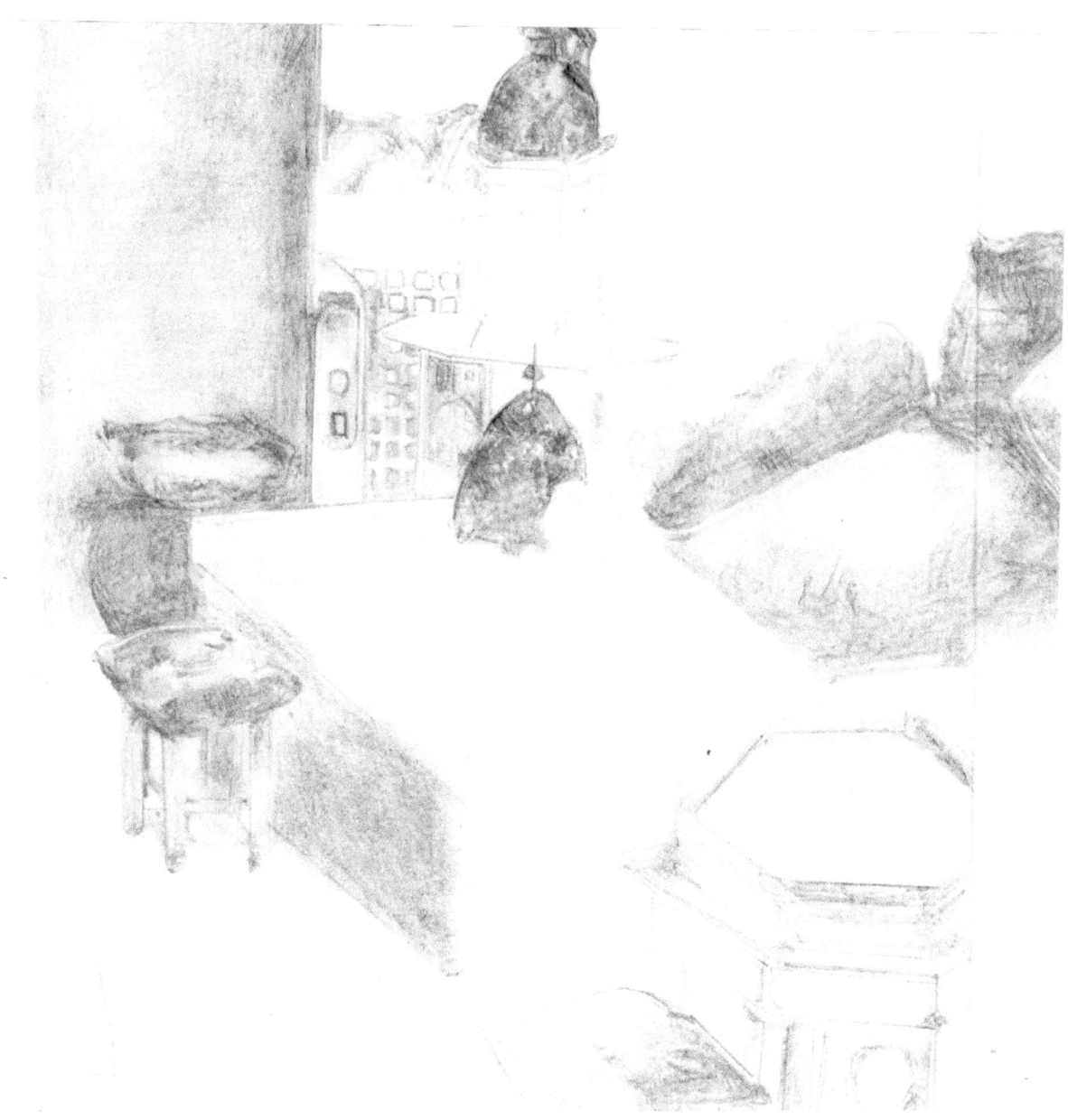

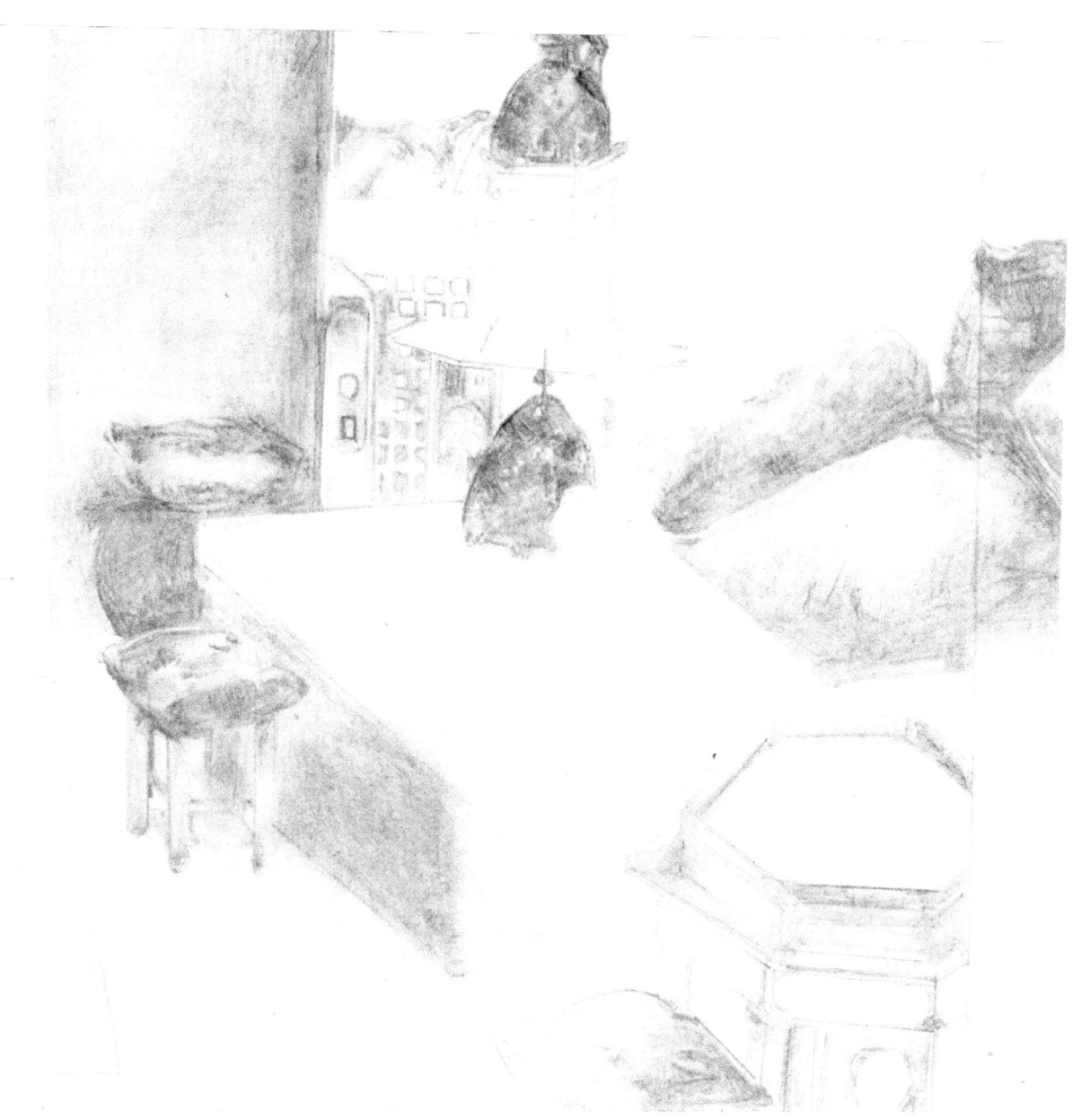

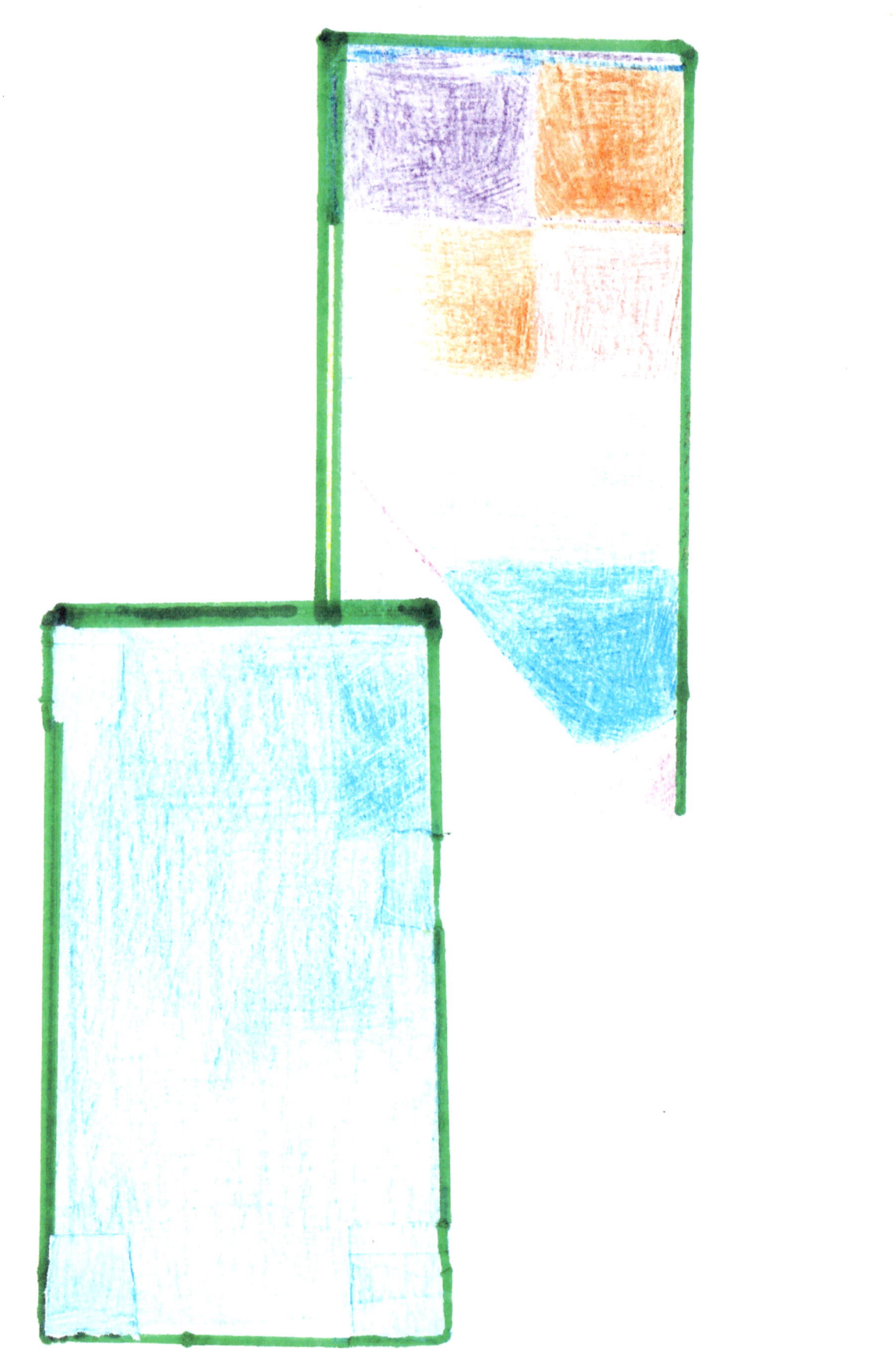

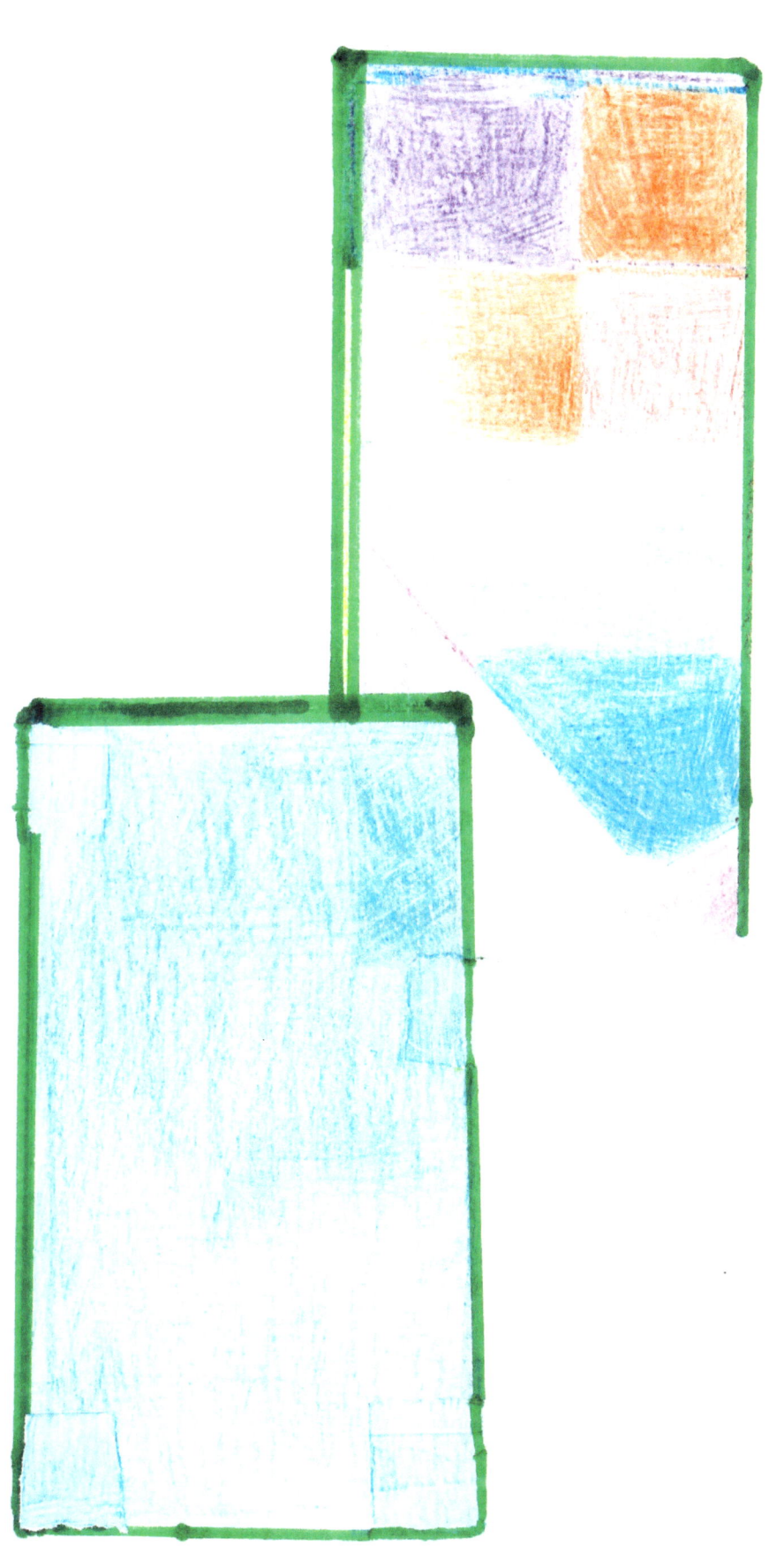

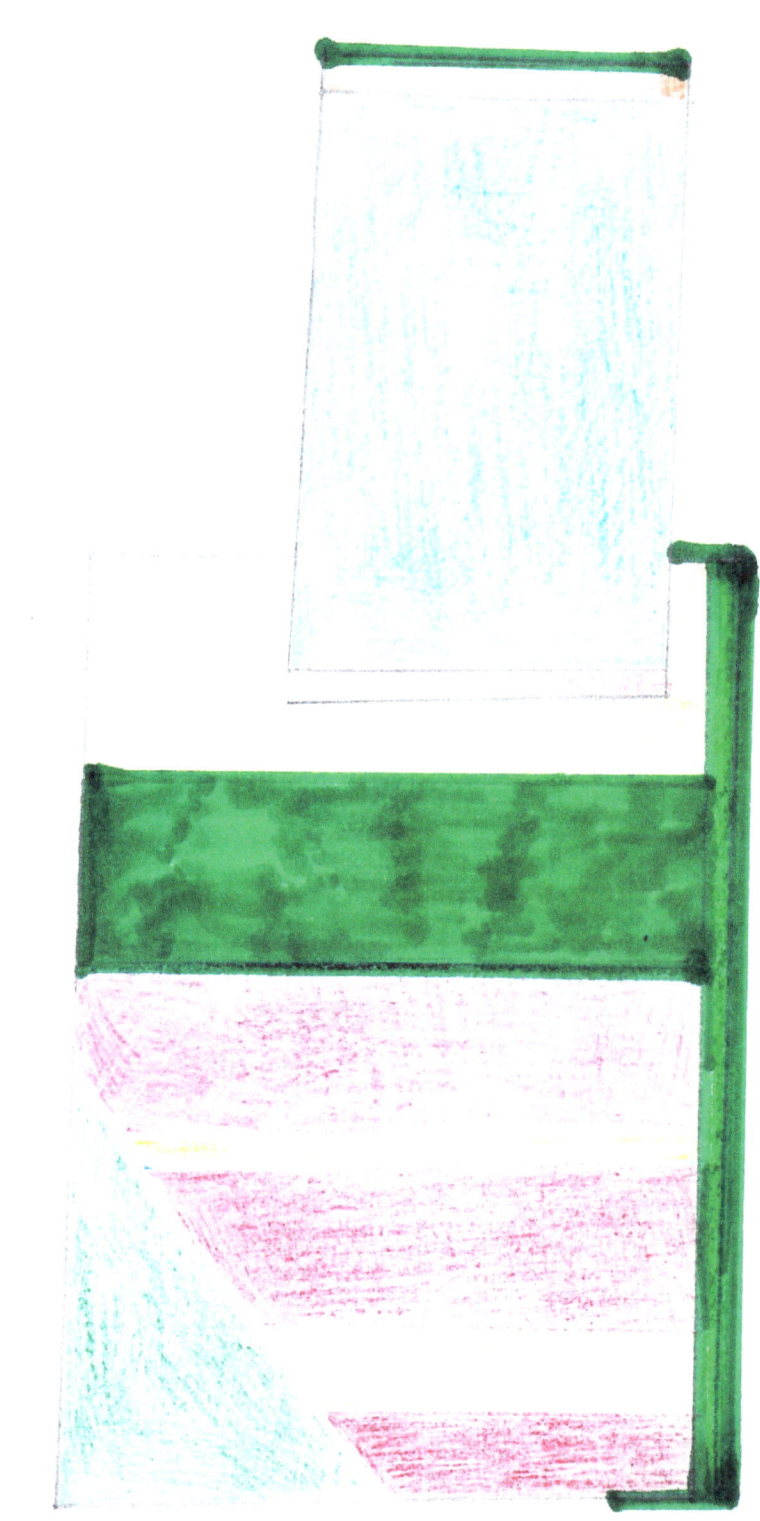

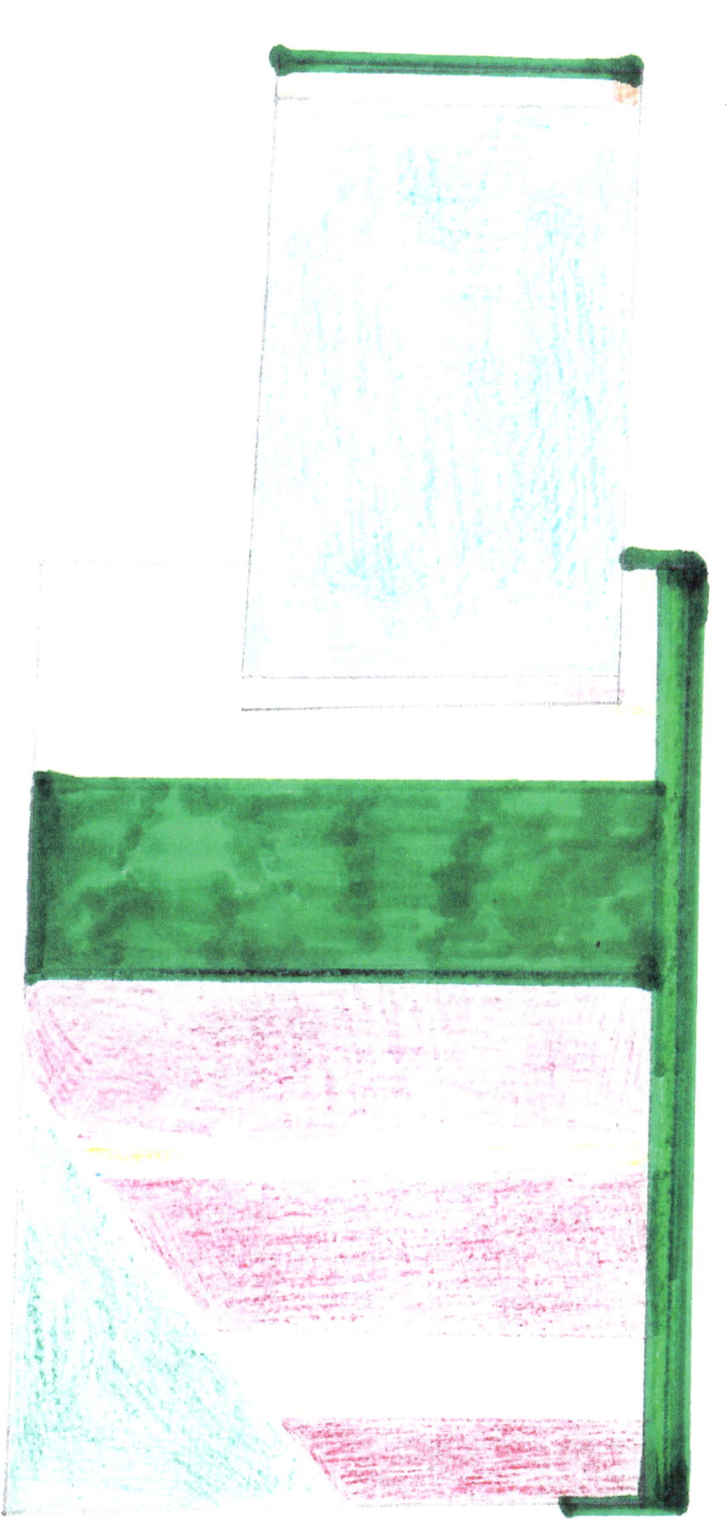

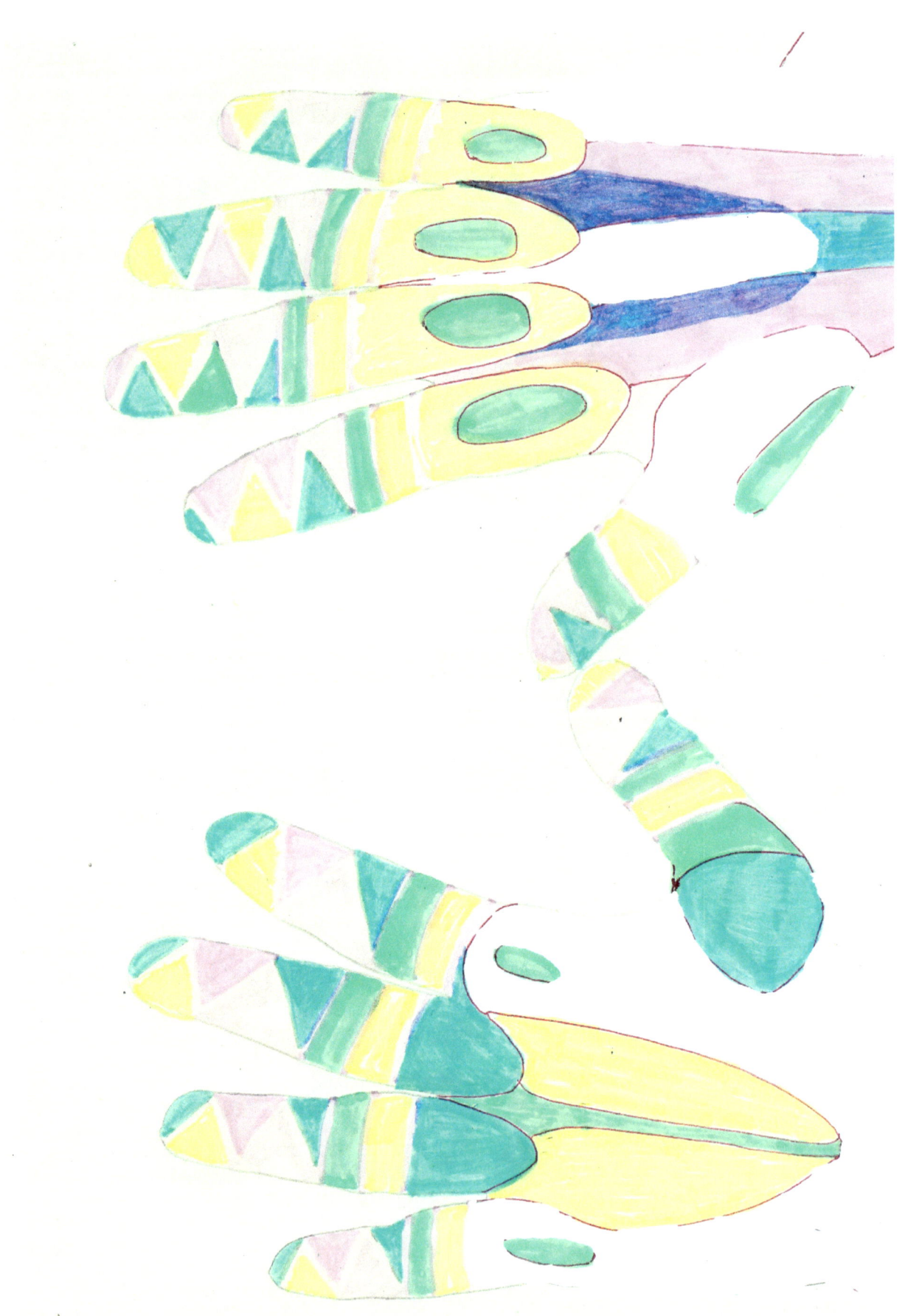

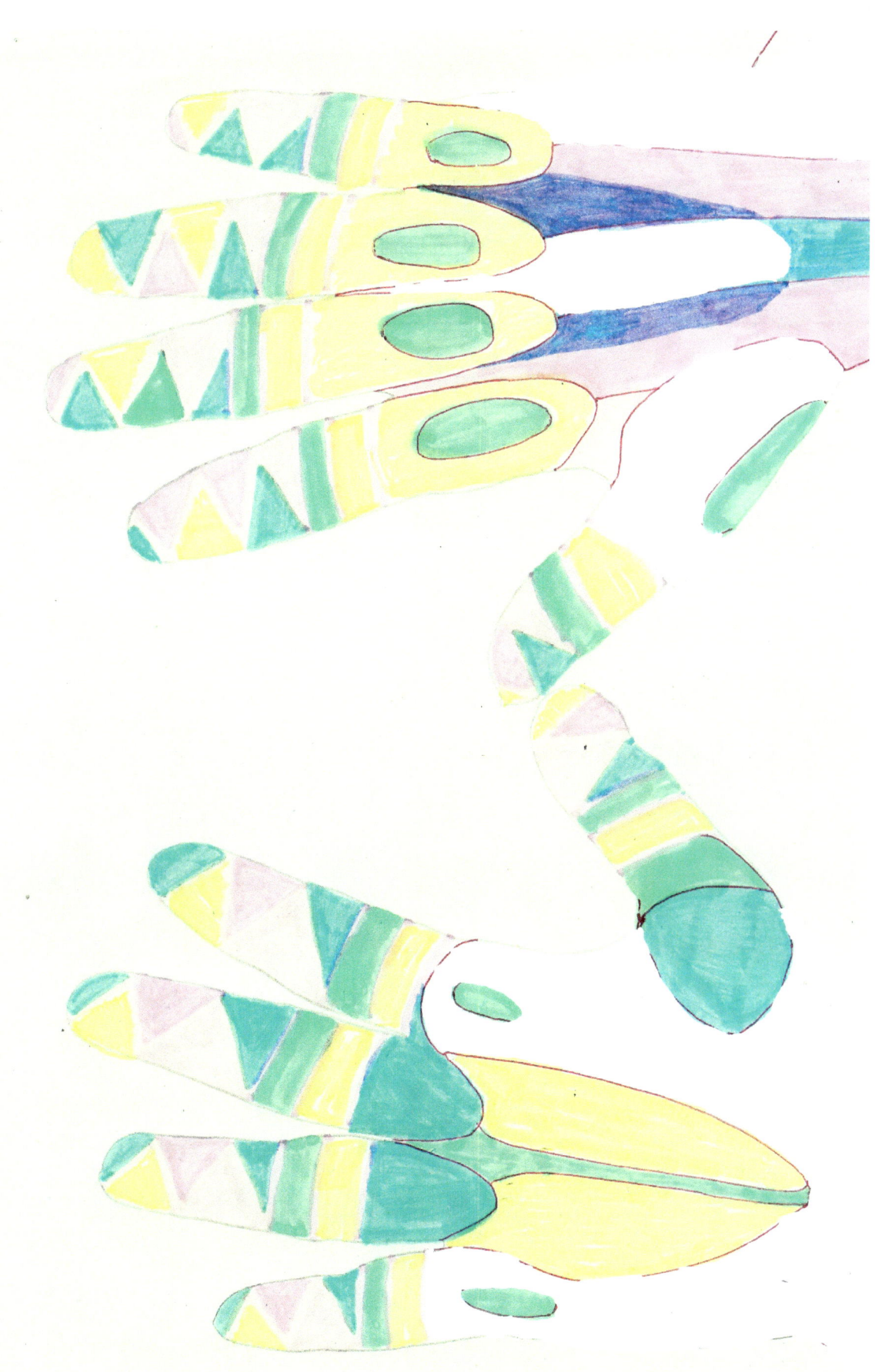